Pretenders

Books by Jeff Friedman

The Record-Breaking Heat Wave
Scattering the Ashes
Taking Down the Angel
Black Threads
Working in Flour
Pretenders

Pretenders

poems by
Jeff Friedman

Carnegie Mellon University Press
Pittsburgh 2014

Acknowledgments

My thanks to the editors of the following publications in which these poems first appeared:

American Poetry Review ("Give It Up"); *Anthem* ("Note to Self on Getting Fired"); *Blue Lyra Review* ("Old Bird" and "Tea"); *The Drunken Boat* ("Regret," "Story of the World," and "Brokers"); *5 AM* ("Dusk," "What I Learned from the Animals," "Money," and "Rat in the Closet"); *Margie* ("Galicia"); *New England Review* ("Mud"); *Naugatuck Review* ("Breaking the Fast"); *OVS* ("Sitting Shiva" and "Somebody"); *Phantom Drift* ("Snapping Turtle"); *Poet Lore* ("Horse"); *Poetry International* ("Pretenders" and "Not Babs"); *Prose Poem Project* ("Pill"); *Salt Hill Literary Journal* ("Wine"); *Sentence* ("Judges"); *Solstice* (The Y Chromosome" and "How Empires Fall"); *Spillway* ("Five Brothers," "Bear Fight," and "On Sex"); *The Spoon River Poetry Review* ("Spreading the Son," "Of Chickpeas and Chickadees," and "About the Ears"); *Storyscape Literary Journal* ("Willem of Hands"); *Sukoon* ("The Great Man" and "Crossing a Border"); *10 x 3* ("Follow Your Bliss"); *U City Review* ("Family History"); *Zone 3* ("Flurry," "Majesty," and "A Word About My Famous Mentor").

The poem "Give It Up" also appeared in *Solstice* and received a nomination for "Best of the Web." "Galicia" reappeared in *Cardinal Points*. The poems "Galicia," "Somebody," and "Sitting Shiva" were reprinted in *The New Promised Land: 120 Contemporary Jewish American Poets*. My thanks to Charna Meyers, Roy Nathanson, Dzvinia Orlowsky, Ken Smith, Jennifer Millitello, Howard Schwartz, Celia Bland and Steven Schreiner for their help, insight and encouragement. My special thanks to Judith Vollmer for reading my manuscript, offering her suggestions and providing me with the final structure of the book. And my deepest gratitude to my editor, Gerald Costanzo, for his belief in my poetry and his generosity.

Book design by Stacey Hsi

Library of Congress Control Number 2013937120
ISBN 978-0-88748-579-4
Printed and bound in the United States of America
10 9 8 7 6 5 4 3 2 1

for my beautiful wife, Colleen

Go where the others went to the dark boundary
for the golden fleece of nothingness your last prize

—Zbigniew Herbert

Contents

Three

Four

Mud

Out of the river, mud climbed
broken embankments, crooked staircases,
gleaming hulls, the corpses of cows,
the skulls of cars. Out of the river,
mud entered our homes, roasted
its dinners in our ovens, filled our glasses
with gritty wine. At night, it made our beds, tucking
sheets and spreading covers. Mud said
its prayers and wept for us. It ticked in our clocks.
It wore our shoes and socks, plastered our ankles.
Mud took over banks, gas stations,
the mayor's office. Mud baked our bread.
It spoke a thousand tongues, translated
our deepest needs into simple sentences.
It filled out our forms, smudging the signature line.
When mud wavered, even for a moment,
it kneeled in soggy churches, renewed its faith.
With its conscience clear, mud mixed
its own cocktail and went out to spread
the word, its logic impossible to rebut.
Mud drove a convoy of trucks unloading
cargoes of itself. Mud dammed the flood.
It hired us to work, raking mounds of it
into gardens and carrying it in pails.
When we looked up, even the sun was mud.

One

After the Flood

for Brenda Garand

A week after the flood,
Betsy and I work on Brenda's tools
while she pulls out drawings
too damaged by water and mud to repair
and throws them outside
to be taken to the dump.
She's already filled one large
truck with ruined sculptures,
already lost more than a hundred pieces.
The garage door is wide open,
letting in warm dry air.
The walls, scrubbed with bleach, almost sparkle
though they are permanently stained.
Betsy and I spray penetrating oil
on calipers, wrenches, screwdrivers
and when the gold foam dissolves,
we scour the tools with steel wool
until we've removed as much rust as we can.
Outside, the bright sun
shines on mud-caked walls,
posts, and signs, shines
on the faces of families in West Hartford
who camp out on lawns
in front of their gutted homes.
"If the water rises into the barn,"
the fireman told Brenda
the night of the flood,
"climb onto the railroad tracks,
because no one can get to you

until morning." She watched her
house fill with water
and her propane tank float down river,
swept away with a whole raft of propane tanks.
Only a short while ago,
she was in tears, her emotions
too large to control. Now
she laughs as Betsy and I
do a mock testimonial for the Blaster,
laughs as we sand down tools
and place them on white towels
to dry out. Only some of them
can be saved.

Galicia

In Galicia an elephant scratches the ear of a flea,
and pigs wallow in broken clouds. In Galicia
I smear my face with the juice of celandine stalks
and climb a tree, surveying the rubble.
In Galicia water swirls and swirls.
Horsemen swing their angry torches.
Couches are filled with dung. The forest of diamonds flickers.
In Galicia I wrestle a rooster for the right to the bones.
In Galicia three heavy white horses drink tea without me.
Rain flies sideways, feathers drifting over an empty bed.
In Galicia a crow caws over the rooftops.
In Galicia my grandmother kisses me on the forehead,
twisting the dough for her famous knishes.
My grandfather leans closer to the Talmud, squinting his eyes.
In Galicia the piano benches are hopping while the count prays for rain,
and saints bathe their decapitated heads,
before robbing the tombs buried in the walls.
In Galicia I bake bread for the empress, who honors me with a ruby.
I hum to the earth where my ancestors lie. Hair grows
on the graves. Flies swarm my head.
In Galicia I ride against the Cossacks, waving my saber.
In Galicia I strike a match and fire rises to the sky.
In Galicia the pogrom starts at midnight.
Roses bloom under the moon.
The muddy river blasts white rock.
In Galicia I sleep in a coffin, and the crow
smells the flames long before they are burning.

Majesty

When her Majesty walks into the room, all emeralds and rubies, when she executes her dazzling curtsies and opens her sumptuous arms, we kneel and wait for her to occupy her throne. Once seated, she orders us to rise and takes a head count. Now we're missing Nils, the Swiss Chocolate ambassador; Magenta, once her principle lady in waiting who lost her head in hot pink; Giles, the court scribe who told the truth only once before he disappeared; and Geronimo, her forgetful lover, who forgot her one too many times. We're happy to be alive, happy the warm rich sun of the palace shines down on us, happy her Majesty pours out her heart to us. She only wants to be loved. She only wants to rule with wisdom. When her scepter strikes the air executing a city of flies or calling for rain or decreeing a war on frogs or taxing another country of anthills, when she looks to us for counsel, we sing her praises. The country has fallen into poverty and gloom. We've strained the water and dirt for every last precious metal, and now the water is fouled and the dirt is depleted. The witches say that only the darkness will survive us. We say, "Majesty, Majesty, Majesty . . ."

Horse

Give me a horse, he said, so we gave him a horse; only now he needed a paddock so he could parade the horse, so we gave him a paddock; only now he needed a saddle, so we gave him a saddle; only now he needed a leg up, so we lifted him by his boot; only now he needed a racetrack, competition—other jockeys and horses—and a crowd, so we gave him all of it, and he took off flying around the track at a record pace; only now he needed a finish line and cameras flashing, so we gave him a finish line and the cameras aimed in his eyes; only now he needed a trophy to lift over his head and a big pay off, so we gave him the trophy and a big pay off to boot; when he turned around, the money was gone. He pawned the trophy for pennies. When he returned to the track, it wasn't there. Give me a horse, he said; so we stuffed a bit in his mouth and spurred his sides until he took off in a mad gallop; now he didn't even need us.

Old Bird

Old bird is creating a commotion again, flying around the room with his big stinky wings as he rages on about injustice. "Buy now, suffer later," he shouts. Feathers fall over us, sticking to our shoulders and faces. "Come down," we say. "Have a bite to eat." "Not until the time is right," he answers. "The time is right," we say. "Besides you're not an angel." "I'm a prophet," he says. "You look more like an angry bird," we say. Now he's bumping the walls and the ceiling. Plaster comes down in pieces. On his next swoop, he causes the light fixture to crash on the floor. I toss some pellets into the corners of the room. "Food for thought," I say. He eats them like cookies. "Got anymore?" he asks. The stench in the room is so strong we cover our noses with our shirts until one of us grabs him from behind, and then we strip his wings and toss them in the trash. "You won't be needing these anymore." Without his wings, we can see clearly his bloated belly and the ugly expression on his face. "I'm a prophet, he says as we truss his legs, stuff him with onions, and put him in the pot.

Noah's Last Note

Let's not forget the greased pig,
how fast he gobbled down the dogs
and took off into the tall weeds
where the wedding went up in smoke.
Let's not forget Basia, her singed
frock falling into the puddle at her feet
as the chimp cartwheeled from branch to branch,
pollen coating his fur, as the kites stole
dolls out of the cribs—a thousand dolls
with pudgy faces floating over our blue avenues—
as the serendipitous surrenders gave way
to the oven bird's mockery, and overabundant
ovaries delivered their eggs promptly
at 11 before the haze set in, before the bees
went on a rampage, and sunflowers lost their heads,
before the azaleas were born, before the stags flew
out of the stagnant pools, before the frogs
forged a new alliance with the snakes
and honey oozed from all our sullen places,
before the bankers absconded with the vaults,
before the wizened patriarchs sold off
cemetery plots of cyberspace, before
all the books became bits
and fish bloated in underwater camps,
before the doves betrayed us with their white wings,
before the dolls began exploding
while waves rose higher and higher—
the ark sailing blind into the blaze.

Our Dictator

Our dictator carries a sack
of grievances and tosses them in air
and some of the grievances
fly over us like pigeons
and some fall like ash
and some fall like confetti
and some sparkle like polished coins
and some bob on a gust of wind
like puppets
and some disintegrate like words.
Our dictator praises the kites
trailing their tails
over the avenues. He waves
his arms, and tsunamis
blow over the oceans,
waves towering over cities,
tossing homes and villages
into compost heaps. Our dictator
wrestles the wasted angels
from their lachrymose ladders
and pins them on their filthy backs,
demanding payments. Our dictator
runs with the roosters who scratch
their names everywhere and wink
at the TV cameras as they dance
over glittery ballroom floors.
Our dictator rolls up his sleeves
and promises millions of jobs,
wheelbarrows full of money,
children with straight teeth

and high IQs, islands
for our retirement. When our dictator
sneezes, drones lock in on their targets,
pearly-eyed fanatics raise
their hems off their boots,
special forces decapitate heads of corn
and tomatoes burst on white fields.
When our dictator sneezes,
his wives blow from his bed
and the windows shatter
and doors burst off their hinges
and bread rises on the roiling water
and the dough catches on the pant legs
of brokers hugging their laptops
as they race back to their furrowed fallacies,
eager to tap Submit and capture another fortune,
catches the puffy hair plodding toward the future.
When our dictator sneezes,
the whole country says, "Bless you,"
as everyone dives for cover.

The Names

When he wrote down Yael's name, she disappeared. We searched for her in the hallways and in her room, but there was no trace of her anywhere and pretty soon, we forgot her. When he wrote down Enoch's name, Enoch blew out like a candle, wax hardening into green coins on the floor. Jared lit a match and burned off the rest of Enoch. When he wrote Esther's name, a dozen men appeared out of thin air, driving a wedge through us as though we were less than air. They overturned the tables in the cafeteria, trapping her against a radiator and binding her hands and feet. She never came back. When he wrote down Jared's name, he grew pale and yellow, the hair floating off his head, strand by strand. Then he wrote the rest of our names down on his table, and some of us fell into manholes and some of us dissolved into dust and some of us turned to echoes ricocheting off walls, and some of us rose into the clouds and rained through the cracks in the building, and some of us descended as pillars of fire burning our names into the walls, recording his crimes.

The Truth Twice

Say the truth once
without any embellishment,
without first qualifying it
so many times even the fog
grows groggy
listening to you
and somebody has to leave
the room or lie
down on the couch
and sleep for a week.
Say it once
and the light'll never
seem so bold as it beams
in your eyes, as you hold
each sweet word in your mouth
and taste it over and over
until your tongue grows numb
from the sweetness
and you feel a little dizzy
with power until your lover,
your wife, your friend
flee your house
made of sand or straw,
or strands of cloud, your house
already melting,
and the spider emerges from
its web, hugging the wall—
full in the belly,
happy to have trapped another.
But say the truth twice

and it'll grow bald
as a lie revealed
as the prophet railing on a bridge
to the empty river
before he takes his last leap
into salvation,
bald as a patient
wasted from her cocktail,
and the cave in your belly
will swell with hollowness.
Say it twice
and a hawk will plunge
from the sky to rip
the hair from your scalp,
and your dog will turn on you,
your teeth will loosen
and your mouth will turn gray
and a pit will open at your feet
and while others crowd around you,
urging you to let go,
somebody will hand you a shovel
to bury yourself.

Brokers

If you want to know the future,
ask a broker. They glow with prophecy
like radioactive birds.
When they meet each other on the street,
they radiate the odor of wealth,
hugging like refugees who have just found
someone from their extinct village.
Money travels fast, so does bad news from brokers.
They steep themselves in oil, pipeline it to sealed tanks
and let it sit as they wait for the markets to crash
and the freeze to begin. When they go home
there are no homes, only a palace or two
with electric gates and motion sensors that detect
even the slightest movement of the poor.
Brokers hum like bats emerging
at dusk, zinging through air
to snag their bloody bonuses. Numbers roll,
heads fly. Confetti rains over suits
as the skies light up with bombs and missiles
and countries disappear from screens.
Brokers win wars, empty
graves so they can fill them again.
They FedEx their packages of ash
to the bereaved and ask for a signature.
Their vaults grow larger than the equator.

Trust Me

From "trust me"
came the church of appalling clauses,
requests for large donations
multiplying like diseases,
came the causes marching
from the dumpsters, the fat palms
waving wads of cash, came
the circus of dark intents,
elephants wallowing in mud,
circuit breakers tripping wires,
highflyers tumbling at appalling rates
while the swollen tongues gathered dust,
while knees fell into disuse,
while knives whittled bones to a whistle,
steak flambéed to a crisp
on the flaming tables, while the waiters
with bristled brushes swept away the remains,
came the tanks collecting taxes
and new exclamations of faith,
brokers stretching their vowels
above countries of electronic transfers,
investments blinking in cyberspace,
came the monkeys twirling batons
in silver bateaus, bats radaring
profits to casinos built in guano
as ministers high-fived their jive,
as genes rose and fell on spirals of DNA,
as angry cells came back to haunt us,
avatars splendid in their regalias of spleen,
as surround sound blared on the bleary horizon,

came the queen who flipped her lid
over the jack of hearts and slid into the funnel,
came the sassy sentences blowing brass,
and all the gods and goddesses
quick as a quake and treacherous to the bone.

Somebody

Somebody breaks a door,
a shadow stepping out
as if to retrieve the morning paper.
Somebody smashes a bottle,
green eyes glinting in the street.
Somebody lets down her hair
and looks in the mirror
at the wrong time and lies
down in the tub, wrist opened.
Somebody reasons with his pain
as if he could strike a deal,
a working arrangement,
and the pills wait counting the minutes.
Somebody recalls the old master
pleading for death
while the young boy plunged
from the sky, his plumage in flames.
Somebody raises a knife
at God's command
and somebody sprays bullets into the bus
before it tumbles off the road.
Somebody snuffs the crow
prophesying a century of famine.
Somebody executes a parrot
for spitting out seeds.
A fire walks down the mountain.

A wave kisses the smoldering moon.
A big wind blows away another city.
Somebody tosses a bomb
in the burning bush
and nobody's talking.

Money

Some of it flew away
when the weather cooled,
clustered in Mexico with the monarchs.

Some dropped out of our pockets
when we weren't looking and stuck
to soles and heels clacking over pavement.

Some grew hot and sweaty
sitting naked in the steam
rising from potholes.

Some died in pocketbooks
or in mouths chewing the fiber
down until it passed

through the esophagus into
the alimentary canal where it was acid-
washed and cleansed.

Some dreamed an empire,
green and shiny on the hill
a palace with gates and guards.

Some smelled of shit and straw
flies swarming over it, laying
their eggs.

Some lay like corpses
in the back of a truck,
waiting to be shoveled into a pit.

And some howled in ash
and bone. The vaults opened
and the banks floated off.

Some sent messages
from faraway islands,
numbers blinking on monitors,

while we typed in new passwords
so no one would steal
the emptiness from our accounts.

The Serpent

The serpent slides on his belly
through the spongy grass. He sings
to you, but his song hisses.
He prays for your health
in a hundred languages,
but the prayers die on his split tongue.
He tosses salt into the wind,
and the salt burns your eyes.
He calls you a snake, remembering
the details of your past
as if it were his own, how
you crawled out of the water
and shed your skin
how you stood up
and walked on two legs.
You walk on two legs,
but you don't fool the serpent.
You believe in angels;
the serpent believes in pigs with wings
wallowing in dusky clouds.
He translates wisdom
into profit, folly into wisdom.
He throws your net into the waters
causes the fish to go belly up.
The serpent picks off
frogs from fronds. He delivers
the bad news to the newts
and salamanders. He retches up
whole tribes. He winds up
the trunk of a tree

and drops on you like a storm.
The serpent shoots through the wind
like an arrow. He frees your blood
with his fangs. He fills up the spaces
where you are missing.
The serpent offers you a deal
on an apple, "Take it," he says.
"It won't eat you," but it does.

Willem of Hands

With his huge hands, Willem squeezed the life out of the butter, greasing the floors and counters. He wrung the necks of cash registers until they were out of cash, out-touked the toucan, taking him for his feathers, debriefing and debilling him, squished the hams into pigs and squared the knots of noggins, knocking sailors out of their sapphire nests. With his huge hands, Willem whaled the tar out of tarmac tailors, stilled the snafus hustling on corners, pickled the pythons raising their dangerous heads into the trees, hulled the gators in the swamps, hugged the crocodiles so tightly they cried real tears. Willem wasted the waddlers and well-wishers, unreasoned the reasoners, pruning them into raisins, ripped the laces out of a thousand languages, leaving millions of homeless morphemes humming for help. With his huge hands, Willem beat the daylights out of rocks and boulders, turned them to dust and debris. He snapped out flames with his fingertips, king konged his lovers so they fell from great heights. With his huge hands, Willem snatched Jonahs from the bellies of whales, snagged sharks on pikes, and slapped the hell out of devils until they were tender as babies. But he couldn't grab the continents before they banged against each other. He couldn't contain the earthquakes or push back the tsunamis. He couldn't grab the stars shooting over his head. He couldn't maul the moon winking at his sister. He couldn't hold the oceans in his palms. He couldn't snooker the world waiting to waste him.

Two

What I Learned from the Animals

When I spoke to a cow
in Yiddish, she answered with a belch,
and some low deep syllables that spread over
the field like gas or pesticide smoke,
but as I turned away, I thought
I heard her mutter the word, "Schmuck."
Flies followed me, but I swatted them off,
except for two with round blue bellies
who clung to my cheeks. In the yard,
chickens strutted past me
pecking the ground and writing
their ridiculous names in the dust:
Alsace, Mingus, Callebaut, and leaving
behind a legacy of feathers.
When I came to the table
with a tribe of hawks, they taught me
to eat small rodents and signal
with a high *e* when danger approached,
but when I began to sing, the hawks
dive-bombed me, dropping their missiles.
"You're hopeless," they said
as I washed my hair on a rock
and ditched my smelly clothes.

And then moose and deer wandered
through the ravine, ripping up hostas
and long grasses, chewing and chewing.
"Get down on all fours," they said. "Eat, eat."
When I did, they laughed. "You're a fool."
And later I vomited up greens for hours.
When I sauntered into streams,
fish came to the surface as if asking to be eaten
and then nipped my ankles.
When the crows read from their book
of prophecies, I fell to my knees
and then one of them blessed me,
waving his wings over my bowed head
while another picked my pocket
and another dragged me through paradise
and left me with a pack of dogs.
"He stinks," they said and bared their knives
and began their feast.

Bear Fight

When Liza fell in with the bear, I was more than disappointed as I had been in love with her since childhood. "What's he got that I don't?" I asked as we walked past the diner together. "He's a bear." She let go of my hand. "He gets a little jealous when I'm out with my friends." "Why do you want to be with a bear anyway?" Two teenagers pushed past us with their skateboards. Balloons floated above Main Street, announcing a sale at the furniture shop. "Why do you want to be with me?" she asked. We parted ways when the light changed, but later I went to her home dressed as a bear. She opened the door. "Come in," she said, putting her arms around me. "You don't smell like a bear," she said. Then in walked the bear, with a fierce look on his face. He growled and so did I. He cuffed me, so I cuffed him back. Then we grappled with each other, bear-hugging until Liza stepped in between us and held out her hands. "I'm sick of bears," she said. "Get out of here." I ripped off my bear mask. "I'm not a bear," I said. The bear ripped off his. "I quit this game," he said. "I'm not a bear either." Liza removed her mask, and she wasn't Liza. We ran away as fast as we could. I made it back to my place and locked the door, turning on the outside light, but all night I heard her huffing.

On Sex

"Start without me," she says
and removes my hand from her thigh.
"I'll catch up later."
I fall back on my pillow
contemplating my next move.
The TV pops on. Outside chipmunks
kick up their heels, dancing away
with a fortune in acorns. Crows
blast their off key trumpets, signaling
the whereabouts of the fox while chain saws
slice away at white pines and birches.
Just as I snuggle up to her again, hoping
to press against her strategic zones,
she erects a barricade of pillows.
"No sex without intimacy," she states
with great certainty, and the word "intimacy"
stuns the faces of the stuffed animals propped
up in their chairs and beds.
"No intimacy without sex," I reply
and a cluster of red fuzz drifts over us.
But sex is no longer easy; "it takes a village,"
she says. "It takes a country," I answer.
"Let's harvest our vegetable love," I say.
"Let's roll our pleasures into a ball."
"I'm in the mood," I say
and imagine her delicious dish of eggplant and zucchini.
"A kiss is just a kiss," she says
and kisses me on the cheek—I catch
her lips. But I'm funny that way.

Fiction Assignment

"I didn't read the story, " Carly admits,
searching through our small fiction anthology—
authors listed alphabetically—
"because I couldn't find it."
The crows in the back get a kick out of this one
and give her a round of applause.
Blue butterflies stream through air,
and trees lean into the window.
"Let's go outside, " Lauren says,
"I can't concentrate in here."
Above, on the third floor, sirens blare
and gangsters blast their guns.
When Cagney goes down in a hail of gunfire,
the entire film class stomps its feet on the floor.

"Anyone else not read the assignment?"
Everyone in the class, except Rona Winestaff,
a slender waif with glasses much too large
for her face, raises his/her hand.
Three pages: Is that too long?
 "I had a soccer match," Scott says.
The coach kicked him off the team weeks ago.
"I skimmed half of it," Ian volunteers,
"Does that count? He holds his book up
high for everyone to see.

"Let me tell you a story," I say.
"Once I fell in love with a swan who thought
she was a duck. She paddled out
on the lake just like the other ducks,

trying to look like a duck."
"Professor Friedman," Rachel Blankner interrupts,
you're lying again," She cracks open
a bag of chips for her low blood sugar
and begins crunching. In the back
Alexandra lets out her long radiant hair:
"I love a prince," she says.
"She means a drug dealer," Scott cracks,
"who thinks he's a prince."

"I would call to her from the bank,
but she was too much of a duck to be a swan
and I was too much
of a frog to be a prince or a duck.
But one day the swan
peered into the water
and saw that she was a swan.
Then she married a duke—"
"What's a duke?" Scott asks.
"A bulldog, you dope," Jared answers, "like on Disney."

"And one day a princess dropped
her red ball into the water
and a huge talking frog hopped
out and cut her a deal—
one red ball for a kiss—"
Rachel blurts out, "Professor Friedman,
that's another story."

The Y Chromosome

When my friend calls from the West Coast,
he tells me about his blurred sexuality,
his confused Y chromosome, floating
in a gray jelly, deficient in androgen.
He's got a list of all the famous women
who are really men, and the famous men
who should be women.
I've got a list of all the secret anti-Semites
including the Jewish professor
who teaches Holocaust studies,
but identifies a little too closely with Himmler
and the guy at The Outdoor Shop,
who insisted there was nothing wrong
with the shoes I returned—sole unglued—the problem
was my feet. "At this age," I say, "We're all a little
uncomfortable in our own skins."
Near the table, my dog thinks she's a deer,
letting her ears rotate like antennae
and bounding away from me.
And a stray gray cat pretends to be
part of our family, lounging
on the dog's futon outside on the deck.
Though he dresses in dresses
and his face has grown round and soft
from the hormones, my friend still only loves
women's bodies. I love women's bodies too,
I think, but mostly from memory.
Now my friend talks about how he wants
to make love to this woman he has known for years,
the wife of one of his closest friends.

"Dave doesn't understand her," he says.
I'm pretty sure that's his testosterone
kicking into gear, even if his "Y" chromosome
appears to be wading in the wrong pool.
As we talk, cells are reproducing
by the billions, even trillions,
male and female genes combining
and recombining until fish walk
out of the waters, lizards roll
over in sand, until dragons again
breathe fire into weightless windows,
and dinosaurs dally in the tall grasses,
the world pumped full of sex
and not a thing we can do to stop the onslaught,
except wag our tails and race upstream
toward the white rocks.

Crossing a Border

Say what you want.
The bridges are buckling,
the roads collapsing,
18 wheelers tumbling
with their cargos of hazardous waste,
their casks filled with poisonous wine,
their drums leaking.
Clouds blossom, pink and fat.
The sky smacks us in the face.
Say what you want.
The knots are failing,
the houses coming loose.
The finches turn up dead,
while foxes behead our stunned chickens
and gutted cars rust in the ravines
and moose linger by the shoulders of the roads,
licking up the salt runoff
and bears tear off bark
to get at the ants,
and tiny spiders bite
into our fleshy feet
and tumors populate our townships.
Say what you want: cities of tents
and sheets multiply across the globe
while cows shrink to stamps
and famines grow too numerous to count
and the stalks rise and fall
and skin tightens around bone,
red eyes glinting at the gates of palaces,
villages incinerated, armies

of flame burning up the air.
Say what you want.
Bankers and brokers own the poppy fields,
the drug dealers,
the men on camels
with automatic weapons,
and missile throwers
and anti-missile detection systems.
They own the cells hidden in caves,
the coca leaves, the machetes,
the tsunamis, earthquakes,
vaults the size of equators,
the rigs plunging into ice,
the vast storehouses of oil
locked in rock.
Say what you want.
We're all refugees from our homeland,
fleeing countries of pain.
We're all crossing a border,
dying to get in or out.

Of Chickadees and Chickpeas

Yes, female chickadees often settle down
with a single partner, but if their spouses
fare poorly in the local singing contest,
they've been known to take off
before dawn for a vacant tree
a good distance from home
where they hook up with a leading vocalist
—whose feathers are bright and shiny,
freshly preened—for a thirty-second tryst.
But let's not confuse the chickadee
with the chickpea, which really has no choice
about what stew it winds up in. And let's not
forget that men who cook for women
often charm their wives into bed
even after years of marriage,
that is, if their wives don't wind up
with gas or heartburn.
For some reason the male chickadee
lets the adulteress back into the nest
without questions or recriminations.
Perhaps he's too tired from his own last thirty-second
tryst or from practicing for the next singing contest.
Of course, the wife of the star singer
also displays great flexibility and understanding
as she lets her man off the hook
scot-free but she may be demanding
two or three lovemaking sessions
in the next two minutes because we know
if they're to have children, female chickadees need
to be fertilized, which is much different

from chickpeas, which simply need
to be soaked overnight and cooked
for a long enough time so that they're tender
but not mushy, though some people prefer
them soft—though you say crunchy is best.
Chickpeas swell in water like pregnant chickadees.
And chickadees often call out a sequence
of "chickadedees" with many "dees" on the end
should a fast agile intruder enter their territory.
And that's why it's important to stick together,
because you never know what's around the corner
or what disaster might occur when you least expect it.
The chickpeas are delicious, have another helping.

Try a Little Tenderness

"Try a little tenderness," the old man
sings to his dove.
There's love in the air, thick
as hate, love floating like feathers,
love on the lips puckered and pursed
hiding the powerful canines,
wishing for a bite.
"Try a little tenderness," he sings
and squishes a ladybug
between his fingertips, blood crusted
in his nails. He smells the soup boiling,
remembers how another dove
slipped through his grasp
and smashed into the windowpane,
killing what they had between them.
This dove lowers the flame.
This dove breathes in the smell
of onions, carrots, potatoes,
bay leaves, nutmeg, squash.
This dove readies herself
for another of his bouts with rage,
hunkering down with her knives.
There's love in their mutual disrespect.
There's love in the steam rising
from the kettle, love brimming over,
love in the the blind eyes
of the windows—love
in the precision of the knife
cutting meat from bone.

Family History

My aunt Viola took up with Uncle Charlie in the '50s
after her first husband, a handsome rake, fled
her wild blue eyes and long "suicide-red hair."
She walked with a limp, a bad hip.

She fell in love with Charlie when he got down
on one knee and she could see a tiny bald country
shaped like Hungary. "Everyone there looks like us,
same beady eyes," she always claimed, "and they're all
crazy drinkers or just plain crazy."

Charlie never acted nice to anyone,
but my aunt. He carried a folding chair
over his shoulder for her and opened it—even
on crowded NYC sidewalks—whenever she got tired of walking.

After they died, I found an envelope behind some books
with the word "naughty" scribbled in red.
In the photos my aunt, so modest she wore
a robe over her bathing suit at the beach,
sits naked on the edge of the bed,
as though ready to wave at her nephews and nieces back home.

Charlie is somewhere near the radiator,
telling her to smile and look natural.
If she knew that anyone was looking at these photos
she would rise up and drop dead again.
Their ashes still float on the East River,
bickering like Hungarians.

About the Nose

In front of the mirror, my mother brushed
my sister's thick dark hair
untangling the knots gently and bringing out
the sheen as my sister wept for Harvey Ginsberg

an Orthodox Jew with long curly
sidelocks, who a year before dropped her
because she wasn't Jewish enough.
When she pulled the brush

away, my sister tried to slip her grip
but my mother held her head firmly,
"Get your nose fixed," she said.
"You'll feel better."

My sister stared at her nose, long
and straight, no hook or slope or
budding potato on the tip. From my spot
on the floor, I intruded, "People with small noses

don't breathe as well. It's a known fact."
My mother raised the hairbrush into the light, letting
me know she could use it on me if necessary.
My sister pressed the button of her nose

and now she had a snub nose and my own
long nose, prophet of the air,
smelling the lilacs and the yellow particles
of pollen that floated through the screens,

twitched and twitched until even
my mother cracked a smile
as she handed me a box of Scotties.
Outside a few leaves took a nosedive

and a sparrow landed on the sill, showing off
its perfect schnoz, while I blew and blew
knocking down loose plaster, shaking
the mirror, beating the daylight out of the air.

Note to Self on Getting Fired

Don't be ungrateful
and don't snarl or make
any passive aggressive comments
that begin, "I know it couldn't be helped,
but . . ." as you are prone to do.
Tell your boss you love her
as no other boss before her.
Tell her she has the right
to behave as she does,
sending out secret memos
to those who have survived
yet another cut,
because she's the boss,
and bosses burn like pilot lights,
slow and steady until someone lights them,
and they flare blue and yellow.
Forget karma or revenge.
The boss is ready for another day
and when she calls for help,
help always comes
and another memo fires into cyberspace
as matches flare under piles of leaves.
The smoke never clears,
because the fire is always burning,
and she will remain long after
the ash has drifted away.
When she says "The orders
come from above"
and shakes her head gravely,
shake your head in harmony.

To save jobs, she has to fire
more people, clear a space
for more space,
boxes walking out on their own.
Don't question the logic.
Tell her you appreciate
all the work that went into
getting rid of you and leave her
a handful of hard candies.

Taking It All Off

for Dzvinia Orlowsky

My friend's daughter calls her a hairy beast,
"because I've got a fire patch," she says
and laughs, but she knows that gray
is raining on her fire. I laugh also
because after so many years on earth,
our genitals are no longer
a secret, hidden even from us.
Despite the chafing, her daughter asks:
"Who wants anything but smooth
these days?" Better to be young.
Better to shave it off down
there, go skin on skin.
Get rid of the evidence, even if
you have to shoot your whole body full of Botox.
No more landing strip for the quickly aging,
no brush in which to hide your weapons,
no lovely plush on plush.
Get rid of the carpet. It's musty and old,
probably full of dust mites like the sheets.
Goodbye to the thickets, where sweet birds sang.
Goodbye to the headdress, the hirsute hibiscus,
the fuzzy funk, the filamentous,
fulmination, the huckleberry hotbox,
the parliamentary pussy, the presidential penis
dressed in his weeds. Goodbye
to the drunken dives into the thinning pelt.
Time to get in step with youth,
go for a clean sweep, a wax job
or a deep depilatory—clean as a whistle.

Forget the sweating and the effluvium rising from the skin.
Soon there'll be a spray to sweeten your air.
Bless the pale polyglot, the surly
white head of the scallion, the glabrous gonads,
the pupil, but not the pulpit.
Bless the pearl, the shiny love mound,
the tattoo telling you where to enter.
Wake up! You're at a big wedding party for naked genitals.
Everyone is winking or smiling.

Oral Sex, 1969

"You're a long way from the pearl
in the pulpit," she says,
when I go down on her. But I keep at it,
twirling like a helicopter taken by the wind,
and I remember my father telling me, "Son,
straighten up and fly right,"
wondering if this is what he meant.
She pulls me up through her legs only to lie
next to her. I recall our first nights
of lovemaking, how I hoisted her
against a wall, how we floated
over the wet streets like lovers in a Chagall painting,
like men and women in Kama Sutra drawings,
how the orgasms rolled like dice.
"That was real lovemaking," I say.
"That was someone else," she replies.
I plunge downward and let my tongue
do the talking, and even though I'm feeling
its passion, nothing happens.
I review the steps, where I might've moved
too fast or too slow or pressed
down too heavily or lightly,
but remember reading something about
how it should all come naturally
as leaves to the trees.
Now, I just hold her in my arms
and she seems relaxed, almost happy.
"Who has an orgasm every time, anyway," I say.
"You do," she answers.

Trap

"Time to go to work," Dominique says, but I have no job. As I sit on my chair, I think about what I have to do today and come up with nothing, but Dominique is insistent that I get a move on it, so I rise from my chair, and the door closes. I turn the knob, but it's locked. When I sit down on my chair, the door is open, so I get up again and the door slams shut in my face so I sit down again, "You're late," Dominique says. "For what?" I ask. I sit down again and close my eyes, imagining what I might be late for, but nothing comes to mind. "For everything," she answers. When I wake, the door is open, so I get up again and walk to the door, only this time it stays open. It's a trap, I think and sit back down on my chair, and without a word, Dominique is gone.

Judges

After the guest ate all the potatoes and the whole brisket, after
he ate the tzimmes, the roasted beets and the fruit cocktail, he
called for Elijah to enter the door, for Elisha to send a hatchet
on the water, for Joshua to blow his trumpet. He called for
Moses to drum up more business in this poor economy. He
touched his Star of David. He touched the mezuzah on the
door. Something's wrong, he said. This house has lost its
harmony. What can we do? we asked. He didn't answer.
Instead he ate the chickpeas, the hummus and all the leavened
and unleavened bread. He ate the honey cake and the prune
pudding. What else could we feed him? Would he fix the piece
of Torah nailed to our doorway? Would he bring peace? Would
he boil the pots and pans and say a prayer? Would he rock back
and forth in his white shawl? Next, he ate the porcelain bowls,
plates and all the silverware, then the glasses and tablecloth.
He ate the chairs and the dinner table and then the couch and
coffee table. He ate our phones so we couldn't call for help. He
ate the dust, the particles of debris and shed skin, the shadows
with their long threats, the voices rising from the floorboards,
the blessings that failed to bless. When he finished, when the
place was empty, he looked us over, flashing his teeth. As we
backed away from him, he belched loudly, said a prayer. "That
should take care of the problem," he announced. Now there was
nothing left to fight over, but nothing was more than enough.

Three

Clearing the Roof

for Colleen

For hours, crouched on the roof,
we pulled up mats of moss
with rubber gloves.

My eyes stung. I wiped sweat
from my face with my shirt sleeve.
Then, while I rested, you brushed shingles

with bleach, but some of the shingles
were paper thin. "Be careful,"
I said, "you could tear them off."

When hornets flew up from the eaves,
I waved my arms
wildly as if signaling for help.

"It's like a lawn," I said, ready to quit.
You laughed, but wanted to get the job done.
"Be careful," I repeated,

as you moved closer
and closer to the edge, pulling
up patches of moss

and tossing them onto the patio,
which we would have to sweep later.
A crow and a hawk clamored

grazing each other in mid-air.
"Be careful," I whispered,
and saw how fatigue rouged your cheeks

and made you sink to your knees,
how later in bed
you lay in my arms

too tired to sleep,
as wind crinkled bags of leaves
and night welled up in our window.

It's Blue

You say it's gray like the cat
on the deck rail who lets her tail
tick back and forth
above our sleeping dog
as if attempting to fan
Bekka's whiskers. But even
if a little white has been added
to the mix I call it blue—
blue like some corner of the brain
where nothing gets accomplished
for weeks, not even opening
the mail that is piling up
on the corner of the dinner table
until it slides down and occupies
half the placemats. Maybe,
it's a cloudy blue, but it's not gray
which may not even be a color,
depending on who you talk to.
It's certainly not a pretty blue.
I like the dark blue, almost black,
to the naked eye, of my T-shirt,
which I wear way too often—
which causes you to hint I should
wash it occasionally.
You say it's gray,
and there's a gray area
between colors, a fuzzy border
that might go either way,
depending on hue and value.

And it's hard for you
to hear what I say unless I say it
standing in front of you in the same room,
where I can look into your lovely blue eyes.
And it's hard for me to reach you
when you're working in the garden
so many hours, pulling weeds
and planting new flowers,
as the blue air darkens,
though I wave my arms and shout
and try to bring you back.

Spreading the Son

My son was ash. I cupped him in my hands, tossed him into air. He flew into the trees, flew toward the clouds. He swirled like a swarm of gnats. He puffed up like a peacock spreading its feathers. He caught on nests, caught the wings of predators who plunged into gullies, the whiskers of voles and the red tails of squirrels, caught on the windshields of cars rumbling over the girders of bridges. He clung to the shoulders of the wind carrying him to the river, clung to the cattails wading near the shore, the milkweed gone to seed, the babies rafting between them. "Come back, come back," I pleaded, but I was only a frail light failing at dusk, only a few molecules riding the backs of twigs, only the particles burning in the hand, a handful of salt spreading everywhere like a desert.

Day of Atonement

I didn't repent or atone this year
even though more than a few times
I left mounds of crumbs on the counter,
water splashed on the cabinet doors,
bits of garlic, celery, and onion
dotting the red floor mat just after
my wife had cleaned all the surfaces
and thoroughly vacuumed the floors,
and once I forced my closest friend
to pay for dinner at a fancy restaurant
claiming I had forgotten my credit card
and another time, I purposely forgot
to sign the petition from moveon.org
to stop a bill that would allow
something else bad to become worse,
even though I lied to a friend
so I wouldn't have to take her to another event
where she could network or target
a potential husband
and I didn't visit enough with my friend
who coughs up blood every day
and rarely leaves the house, whose liver
is failing, though I did talk to her
on the phone. And rather than afflict
my soul, I gave my soul a day off,
a little vacation from breaking rocks
in the torturous sun.
I could have fasted, but I was hungry,
and I'm not one of the Jews
who escaped from Egypt.

No, my ancestors never dragged stones
to build anything so noble or inglorious
as a pyramid, a tomb for the ages,
but they did flee from Russia, Lithuania,
Galicia, Hungary and Transylvania,
hoping to escape pogroms, poverty and death.
If fasting would stop a war
or feed a starving child in Chad,
Sierra Leone, the West Bank
or anywhere else, if it would stop
animals from being tortured to produce our food,
I would fast. Before sundown,
My friend Roy called to scold me,
"You should do what Jews do,
fast and go to synagogue."
Instead I sat in Athens Pizza
and ate a pizza with friends
and drank a cheap red wine.
I thought I heard someone humming
Kol Nidre, but it was only
my brain remembering the prayer
against my wishes. As Yom Kippur
slid into darkness, I closed
my own gates with a toast, half expecting
someone to blow the shofar.

Hawk in the Wood

In the bright sun everything
looks cheery, harmonious,
even the hawk surveying the ravine
from a tall maple. I kneel to transplant
a tomato plant to a larger planter.
In spite of the liquid fence,
the deer have destroyed the hostas
and yew bushes, and a woodchuck
has gotten to my butternut squash.
The tomatoes haven't budded yet,
though it's nearly August. "Not enough room
for the roots to spread," my wife says.
I layer in pebbles for water to seep through
and then shovel in dirt and compost.
I tap the planter to get the plant out,
but it doesn't budge, and my wife
catches the branches. "Be careful,"
she says, "they break easily. Hold the planter
upside down, and it'll give."
The crows create a commotion
warning each other about the hawk,
who could be dreaming he is so still.
When I turn the tomato plant over,
it almost eludes me, but I catch it
without breaking the branches or
letting the dirt crumble away from the roots.
I replant it, breaking the tight
dirt around the roots so they can spread.
I feed it some fertilizer, then tie it
to a stick with nylon thread. Except for a few

brown leaves, the plant seems healthy.
In my neighbors' yards green tight
little tomatoes are already beginning to grow.
I've got only a few yellow flowers.
yet my wife tells me there is still hope
for the plants to produce.
A dark net falls over us,
wings pounding the air. The hawk plunges
toward a red squirrel digging
up the dirt, near our tomato plants.
The squirrel eludes the deadly beak by inches,
today too quick for the hawk.

How Empires Fall

It begins with something small:
a virus hitches a ride
on a copter or a few germs
fling themselves into the eyes
of the nurse tending the prince
who drank too deeply
from the fouled water of the pond;
or a flea bites a rat
who scurries into the hold
where his brothers and sisters
cram into the spaces between casks
of wine and the barrels of cured meats;
or something microscopic spews
into the bloodstream and soon
the body wastes away. Of course,
big catastrophes do occur. Asteroids
streak across the sky. Stars collapse.
The planet heats up. Dinosaurs
melt into cave walls. An ice age follows,
but even the worst tempests
begin with a slight stirring in the wind,
and the biggest explosions
come from the smallest particles splitting
or fusing with other particles.
In the end bees drop into the weeds.
The queen becomes listless.
The ant army tramples the poison
and marches back to the nest.
The emperor in mid-sentence
falls off his throne, begging for water.

Or if you're biblical, a black cloud smokes
the invading army. Or maybe in our case,
nothing cataclysmic, nothing special,
will happen at all. The sun'll rise
as it always does, and we'll gulp
our breakfast and watch a quick
snippet of the morning news
before rushing off to work—
teams of analysts with bright smiles
highlighting digital maps
with laser pointers, arguing
over the precise moment
the empire fell.

The Great Man

The great man bullies the fleeces from sheep, the carrots
from the mouth of jackrabbits, the gardens from gods. He
bullies stalks into submission. He bullies the necklaces from
graceful necks, the wings from swans, the fancy shoes from
fancy feet. He bullies flies from spiders, He bullies the birds
from the bush; he bullies the bush until he splits the roots.
He bullies figs, petals wilting at his touch. His tongue never
rests touching his lips, the tip of his nose, licking the velvet
pockets, dulcet wounds, salty cups, Velázquezed veejays.

The great man rules with a firm hand, showing off his rings,
glinting emeralds, ruby reds. He rules with a hoarse laugh,
promises to slay the harried kings, the loose sheiks, the brazen
bulls who question his authority with their bloody horns.
He rules with his own book of prejudice, renames poverty
prosperity, swaggering down the aisles, flowers falling at his
feet.

The great man showers everyone with his bliss. He parts
the rock. He crosses out the sea. He sticks it to his believers
causing them to squeal. The great man banishes his band of
bandits, punishes the pundits who warn him of disgrace. He
hectors the crumpled bodies, rants like an exotic bird in the
wrong paradise, like fire burning up the dry brush, smoke
embracing the ruins.

Failure

The sun rarely comes out,
but when it does
it shines on pink flowers

clustered on rhododendron branches
or the yellow knotted
noggins of peonies,

swarmed by ants, trying to
crack open the skulls.
Why didn't someone tell me

it would be like this, always waiting
for the necessary opportunity—
to do or be what?—

like a dusty piano no one
in the family
has ever played.

Last Call

Here's the box of nothing
you earned over a lifetime,
the orders from above
blasting through a megaphone.
Here are the faces who wish
you hell, and your paycheck
burned with lunch, the sterile stew
of stubs taxed beyond recognition.
Here's the crack in the foundation,
where the building collapses
and the windows fail.
Here's the last call, one
more acetic drink to insure
you reach oblivion. The priests of payola
pump their fists, laugh like pigeons
at your never-ending plight.
The dominoes wait in line,
bills tossed into a hat, fish
flying everywhere, dust
turning into more dust.
Mashed up muses waddle
into the pond for a nude romp.
Here's the final party, the drunk
doors broken off the hinges,
the holy biscuits shredded
in the black basins, the insults
ripping through flesh to bone—
Time to say good-bye
for real.

Wait

for my sister Karen

Today we lean on air.
The cart clatters down the long corridor.
Microwaves heat up towels.
The nurse leaves us alone in the room.

Today the last exhalation comes,
her wizened face letting
go its wrinkles, lips
soft, tongue swollen
against the palate.

Shadows wake up in the alley,
starlings squawk on the wires,
and striped bees
fling themselves through rays,
gold particles falling
into her room, falling over
silvery rails.

Globes of flame blossom
as the sound of our swallowing rises,
as dust settles on our arms,
as the floaters drift into pink
and the bells chime.

Today we recall how she leaned
toward her plate, lifting
her corned beef sandwich
wrapped in wax paper,
with each bite
praising the taste of fat.

Sitting Shiva

I grew tired of the insults,
dishes cracking, phoebes
falling out of their nests,
the little misers who hoarded their coins
as if they were worth something.
I grew tired of wisdom
and those who stood on the ice
looking through the shade,
nodding their heads at misery
and those who came to bring gifts
sympathy, plates of cold cuts, prayers,
who put our house in order,
so I would remember her as she was
or might have been. Instead, I remembered
knives whispering,
nurses in their shiny shoes,
red lines broken on digital monitors.
I remembered her swollen tongue,
cracked lips and torn sores.
I remembered a spot of sun
on black wood, earth falling.

Wine

When I turned the water to wine, Jake complained, "You
turned a bad wine into a worse wine." He sat on the raggedy
bed, his stocking cap pulled down over his ears, belligerent
as always. Under the stocking cap, his bald head came to
a point under some filaments of hair. His blue eyes, once
bright, had almost lost their color.

When I transformed his dingy room, dark and filthy, into
a garden, when I transformed a snake into a staff and beat
the rock until shiny water flowed from it and when the staff
split into flying silverfish, he scoffed. "What's the point?" he
asked. His skin was sallow, and his frail arms hung from his
shoulders.

When I summoned the monarchs to a bright bush, the
sparrows to a hidden tree while the shepherds wrestled in
air and the painted sheep smiled, he nodded, whispering
something I couldn't understand, as if talking to someone
else.

When I ripped his stocking cap off, holding a mirror up to
his face, thick black hair covered his scalp. "That's not me,"
he smiled and fell back into the pillow, his breath misting the
glass.

Tea

When Herkel returned home, his lover had become a cup of black tea. She had been sick for days, lying on the couch with a plaid wool blanket wrapped around her body. He squeezed some lemon and honey into the cup and tasted the tea. "Your lips are cold," she said. He shivered. "Tea doesn't talk," he answered. "I'm not tea," she said, "I'm your lover." He sipped the tea again, still bitter. "Why are you drinking me?" She asked. "I'm cold," he answered. The blanket was crumpled on the couch. He sat down on the couch, pulling the blanket over him. "If you're my lover, why don't you speak to me?" "I'm only tea," she answered. He squeezed a little more honey into the cup and tasted her again. Now she was sweet enough.

Regret

"There's no profit in regret,"
a friend once told me,
a beautiful brunette recalling
the "not so pretty" details
of her numerous affairs.
But what is regret:
a long shadow falling on a sunny day?
a reflection in water?
smoke rising from all the
chimneys of the past?
a room whose objects keep changing?
a city empty except for you?
a scene in the mind
that plays out with infinite variations
but always ends the same?
Regret lives in the heat of the moon
the dark pages of the sun,
among the song of the crickets,
the cries of the cicadas
as they fling themselves toward the sky.
Regret lives in the open hand
reaching out for nothing
it can touch, in the blue
jar of air, in the flicker of light
that disappears before you can see
what you've come this far to see.
But the fox trotting through the ravine
in the early morning sun
regrets nothing
even though the crows

are there to remind him of his murders
and to cash in on the remains.

Dusk

When her hair thinned, when her skin grew paler, I brought
her medicine and hot vegetable soup. She wrapped herself
in an afghan because she couldn't shake the chill from her
body. I sat down next to her and picked up the soup bowl
to feed her the rest of the soup, but she was no longer
hungry. The sun streaked the violet sky a burning pink.
The light blazed in her cheek for a moment and then faded.
I rubbed her feet and hands to restore their heat; still she
shivered. The room darkened. Though I sat next to her, she
seemed farther and farther away, as if islands had drifted
between us. She was disappearing, a memory blinking out
in the mind. I closed my eyes and imagined her voice, warm
as cinnamon at dusk. "I'm here," she said, "here, here, here
. . ." and now there were lights coming on in windows and
houses, spangles glittering in the filaments of her hair.

Rat in the Closet

The rat kept us awake, scratching and chewing, but when we opened the closet door, there was silence. We parted the wall of jackets, coats, shirts, dresses and pants, but couldn't find even a trace of the rat. Then we noticed that my black wing tips had disappeared, and Sabine's rainbow hat was gone. I put down some poison and closed the door, hoping for the best. She didn't like the idea of poisoning the creature. The chewing and scratching grew louder, more persistent. Sabine nudged me to get up, but I was hesitant. "Give the poison a chance," I said. "Maybe it'll move to another apartment," she answered. When the noise suddenly stopped, we waited to see if it would begin again. We both sat up watching the closet door, listening for even slightest hint of the rat, but all we could hear was the sound of snoring coming through the walls and the hum of our own digital clock. "I hope it didn't die in pain," Sabine said. When I opened the door, the poison was still there, but now Sabine's satin robe and my linen jacket had been shredded. There were slivers of wood and chips of paint scattered over everything. We swept up the mess, closed the door, and got back in bed. "Let's leave the lamp on," she said. When we opened the door much later, Sabine armed herself with a hammer. Now the closet was half empty, and we found a hole in the wall. How had we missed it before? I nailed a board over the hole, but knew that wouldn't deter a determined rat. We stayed awake the rest of the night, afraid we might hear the rat return, but more afraid we might not.

Wheels on Fire

"Make it go away," she said. I kissed her forehead, her skin clammy. I turned over my hat, pulling out a thousand silk scarves, all different colors, and tossing them in the air, where they floated. Out of the hat flew a white dove, landing on Julia's lap. She lifted it toward her face, barely able to hold up her arms. The dove disappeared, a single white feather clinging to her palms.

Next, two puppets tangoed in midair, ending their dance with a kiss. A Spanish flamenco guitar player arose from the shadows and played, as a gypsy woman in a red dress took the stage. She raised her arms, pounding her feet and clicking the castanets in her hands, taunting the darkness. Now Julia laughed aloud but the pain started again and tears streamed down her face. I brought her a glass of water and another pill, which she had difficulty swallowing. Then the water became hot brandy with a little nutmeg. "Sip this."

I set in motion four small fiery wheels, spinning like little worlds. Julia smiled and wrapped herself in the afghan as she sat on the couch. She was frail and tired looking, but her brown eyes still had a spark in them. A blue smoke rose from the fiery wheels. The air grew warm, though Julia shivered. With my index finger, I caused the wheels to revolve in a circle like a flaming carousel. "It's beautiful," Julia whispered. When she coughed, I waved my hand until the flames went out, the wheels dissolving into blue smoke, the blue smoke vanishing into my handkerchief.

Four

Salt

Crawling from the sea, salt laid its eggs,
gave birth to pitted clouds, pellets
that glittered in the sand. Salt gouged
trenches, set pipes, poured new foundations,
built cities and houses dense with crystals.
Salt etched its face on paper money,
printing its own currency. Salt bartered with us
for our mortgages, signed our contracts, paid us
nothing out of its own pockets—salting away a fortune.
As it dried our wells, salt dowsed for water.
As it rode the fiery rivers in our veins,
as it spotted our skins, as it stung our tongues,
its grit caught in our teeth, salt
walked in our footsteps, slept in our beds.
Salt hemmed our garments, stitched our shoes.
In our temples, it sang its own hymns,
excoriated our priests and rabbis.
Salt, mourning its brothers and sisters, called
for a minyan, a vote to end all voting.
Salt anointed itself King of the Land,
Queen of the Air. Salt decreed salt sacred.
It smoked our fish, bled our animals,
preserved spirits in jars.It emptied
the banks, started a drought, a depression.
Salt robbed the wind of its tears while it hugged
us tightly, its stars burning our palms.

Good News

Today the mole presses on my forehead
like a determined worm. The orchids
shiver in their bones. There's a sparrow
hopping up a black trunk, a leaf still
dangling on a frozen arm, a crow
ripping into a body, its beak bloody.
There's a train shaking the houses,
a convoy of trucks headed over a decrepit bridge.
A storm wakes inside the mountain,
dust devils twisting into vast columns.
Today, I say a small prayer,
knowing that it can't hurt, a prayer
for my sister-in-law, her blood overrun
by two forms of leukemia, a prayer
for my friend who can no longer leave the house,
coughing up blood, for my wife hunching
in pain, for the heart struggling to pump steadily,
for the cells in our bloodstreams,
for the neurons clustering into brain maps,
a prayer for the sparrow resting outside my window.
Today, on his way to work, Roy calls
from the subway, " Occupy Wall Street's still alive,"
and Fred rising early, calls, "Man, the empire is dead,"
and my sister calls, "It's crazy not to vote."
Here, the world is numb, the ground frozen,
but fires blaze across countries,
and pilots hidden in simulated cockpits in Jersey,
Pennslyvania, Utah, tap their Go buttons
drones unloading bombs over a thousand countries.
And brokers send out giant care packages of debt,

selling off continents piece by piece
as dirty oil spills from fractured rock.
Today, the sun floats over frozen snow.
Email delivers the obituaries.
Good news is far away and travels slowly.

Follow Your Bliss

Joe Campbell said, "Follow your bliss,"
but first you have to find your bliss
and it's sometimes difficult to locate
with all the bling blinding you.
The jangling never stops,
and that too is confusing.
The bus takes you from bus stop
to bus stop not from bliss to bliss.
Rockets crash into craters
on the moon. You can analyze
the debris from now until kingdom come;
you can load all our junk
into NASA canisters—you still won't
find your bliss, let alone follow it.
No, there's more to bliss than meets
the eye. If you kneel before the eye
of the Ayatollah and bless
his blisters, the blessing might
be a kind of bliss unless you smell
his cracked, sweaty feet.
If you bring your yogi some fresh
cut flowers and a few pieces of fruit,
he might hum in your ear awhile
like an energy efficient dishwasher,
but if he knows anything about bliss,
he's not talking. Okay, consult
the Upanishads. That might help
but only if you can read Sanskrit
and don't get involved in the debate
of whether or not Joe Campbell

was anti-Semitic. We're only interested
in "bliss." No, I say forget following
your bliss even for a moment
and you might actually be blissful,
which means you'll be blissed, if not blitzed.

Pill

The father looked at the blue pill on the counter. "You're my son," he said and put his hand on his son's shoulder. "And I'm proud of you, but today you feel powdery and soft like aspirin." The son pulled away. "You're my father," he said, "but sometimes you're a real pill." The father grabbed his son and twirled him like a toy star. "Does that make you dizzy, Junior" he said. "Not on your life. I don't get dizzy." The father poured himself a glass of water and opened a carton of yogurt, digging in with a spoon. "I want to be ready," he said. "You'll never be ready," the son replied. "I don't want to get a bellyache from swallowing you," the father said. "If you swallow me, I won't be your son anymore." The father placed the pill in his palm. "If I swallow you, I'll regain my youth, my strength." "If you swallow me, the son replied, "I'll clomp around inside you like an elephant." The father met his son's stony glare and tossed him down with a gulp of water. He wiped off his mouth. "There are at least 50 more where you came from," he said and shook his bottle of pills, eager to climb the Alps.

A Word About My Famous Mentor

The old man had a few tricks and a few sleeves—under his
sleeves more sleeves, hundred dollar bills taped to cloth,
a deck of aces, silk handkerchiefs, passwords inscribed in
code, maps to stolen treasure with the minefields marked,
his claims to gold mines in Argentina, a cache of rubies and
emeralds, a princess' long tresses—his eyes like arks crashing
into the mountainside, like doves scribbling their names on
blackboards, his eyes like bits of bituminous.

The old man showed me the ropes, looping me into his
loaded vest, like the son he never wanted, licking his lips
like a leopard, lording his fame over all the bank tellers
and waitresses, licking salt from his own lips like a hungry
moose, his mind loping over the tall grasses, flying over
frozen barriers. The old man wasted Hillel, washed away
the Hasidim with their black rags, locked me up with
his homespun wisdom, "Always lead with your chin, take
wooden nickels if that's all you can get, let your hair down
only if you have hair"—the old man lending me the leash to
walk the lizard to the rock, where it sunned all day, catching
flies with its tongue—a flim of a man, flam at his fingertips,
tears blazing at his touch, the tropes tumbling from his
mystical fedora.

The old man danced on a dime, sung the hair back into the
scalp, awoke the flame from molten wax, poisoned the canary
because he couldn't stand the competition, fleeced a squirrel,
walked away with a barrel of acorns, which he traded for
a dozen whole fish, which he traded for a zebra, which he
traded for a dolphin in a tank, which he traded for a Cadillac,

driving through the old neighborhood hundreds of times
until someone shot out his tires. Frail as a lie, flimsy with
his own whimsy, hitting the Enter button on the ATMs,
the old man strutted over the bones of his canards, weeped
and swatted lies from his forehead, wailed at the rabbi,
wringing the neck of a rabbit to show his pain, the old man
ripped through prayers as if chewing grass, a froth in midair,
white moths streaming through the tent, the old man shook
and trembled, happy to put another friend in the grave,
hallelujahed the loudest at the shiva, shivaed at the sound of
his own hallelujahs, then grabbed the last knish and downed
a whole plate of kreplach.

Five Brothers . . .

My first brother and I argued over who should clean the windows. He slammed me against the wall, pushing a squeegee in my face. "Why do we need clean windows with all this damn fog?" I asked. My second brother and I argued over who helped out more at home. "You eat all our food, and you never do a lick of work." He waved his finger under my nose. I laughed and told him that his penny-ante job didn't pay enough to even cover his cigarettes for a week. My third brother drew caricatures of me and pinned them up all over the house. He created a comic strip character in which I was the bad guy, "Ugly Joe," even though I'm not ugly, and my name is not Joe. He drew pictures of me brushing my teeth, sleeping, walking around the house without any clothes, threatening him with a hammer. My fourth brother was a dog. He stole food from my plate and tore up my room if I didn't lock the door. He often bared his teeth, growling at me. Once he tore my best shirt into five pieces. My fifth brother, a parrot, nursed his wounds quietly, but when stirred up would fly into a rage circling the room five times. "Stop repeating what I tell you," I demanded. "Stop repeating what I tell you," he demanded, "what I tell you, what I tell you, tell you, tell you . . ."

Snapping Turtle

When a snapping turtle crawled from the alley onto the
sidewalk, I stopped immediately. Someone had told me that
they're surprisingly fast, even though they don't look fast. I
decided to give it a wide berth and walk around it, but as
I hurried forward out into the street, it blocked my path. I
cut the other way, hoping to get behind it, but somehow the
creature turned quickly enough to prevent me from passing.
I picked up a stick and held it out like a foil, but the turtle
stared at me as if he had no idea what I was doing. Then
I touched his nose with the stick, but before I could pull it
back, he ripped it from my hand, chewing it down to a cigar
stub and spitting it back at me. I felt a hand on my shoulder.
"Excuse me," a short man with a thick red beard said and
walked toward the snapping turtle. "That thing might eat
you alive," I warned, but he didn't look back, and the turtle
let him pass. Then a slender young woman with a lip ring
sauntered by, entering the donut shop on the other side of
the alley. The turtle must be asleep, I thought or turning over
some kind of new leaf. I shrugged my shoulders and headed
by it, but the turtle leaped out, snapping its huge jaw, almost
catching my knee. I backed up, but as I backed up, more
people passed. Then a whole crowd came up behind me,
parting around the snapping turtle, who made no effort to
stop anyone. That's when I saw my opportunity. I fell in with
a group of ten tough looking tattoos, confident that the turtle
wouldn't budge, but just at the moment one of the tattoos
laughed oddly and another tattoo gripped his own neck with
both hands, giving me the choke signal, just at the moment,
it seemed impossible to stop me, the turtle shot out, grabbing
my leg in his jaw and taking me down. Then I grabbed his

neck with my hands, choking him. I cried out for help, but people ignored my plight, some laughing, some talking and some holding their cellphones. The overhead light blinked red and red and red. The Dunkin' Donuts closed up, and the sun slowly faded into evening. When my fingers loosened, the turtle vanished from my grip, leaving me exhausted, alone on my back. As gnats came out in swarms, I righted myself, snagging dozens with my long red tongue.

Story of the World

The world's beautiful with love,
so they say. A dog loves
his master's feet, licking them
until the master puts on
a pair of wool sox; the master
loves the wool sox and his pipe
and the cherry smoke rising
from the pipe, and the cherry smoke
loves its own scent and loves
dust, feathers, shed skin,
gloves of air and the pretty
wind that sings to it while
lovers twist a white sheet
in love with how they love
touching each other until they plunge
into the shuddering sea, surrounded
by tiny sea creatures grazing their legs
and monarchs stream over waves
of breath, returning from South America
as the lovers' bodies glisten
like streaks of fat sizzling in oil,
and their story multiplies for the listener
who waits for the ending
that will unveil the mystery, the truth,
blue flame eating the orange sky,
as the dog now bites the fur
from his legs and the lovers
float toward some conclusion
that neither will love, as the war
explodes on the horizon,

the world shimmering with
the beauty of love.

Innocence

It's something only glimpsed
like a red ball floating on air
gone the instant you turn
or the horse galloping
through a painted cloud
or the boy's sweaty face
as he flies toward the sun
stroking the air
with his wax wings
or the arc of the stone
just before it cracks the skull
and the body falls.
Some say it exists
only in memory, some
say they lost it before
they knew they had it
like a creature shedding
its skin. Some fall
in love with angels
or the eyes of the ingénue
or the young man
with his dream
and bouquet of flowers.
Some love the pink cheeks,
the soft fuzz of the faces.
It comes with a price.
It comes with a red ribbon,
spools of green, a wave
in the air, a bonnet of bees.
It comes with the prophecy

that it will destroy itself
just after it destroys you.
Just when you think,
you've found innocence,
it's gone again like a streak
of flame or a wisp of cloud.
Just when you think,
you know what it means,
it rips into your flesh,
eats you alive.

Outage

When the tomatoes exploded,
the wheat and corn blew toward the sky
and ashes and bits of bone showered over us.

Another country was on fire
and the drought spread like fire
and fire walked on the water,

armies dissolving into salt.
The president unfurled
his secret map of the future.

Minyans of cats voted
against congress, and wild dogs
circled the camps, waiting for meals,

and the crows raised up their armies.
The war bet on itself to win
and cashed in big time,

trillions of dollars streaming
through cyberspace, and then the whole
damn universe crashed.

Old Friends

You find them on the doorstep
crunchy like multigrain pita chips,
crackling with new anger
over something that may not have happened,
or leaning into phone booths
that disappeared years before,
the phone ripped off the cord,
or in the grocery, their leaves
wilted, their shelf life almost expired.
You bag two and take them home with you
for another exercise in misremembering.

You find them sprawled
on couches, clicking the remote,
channel surfing or checking
the hour-by-hour breakdown
of their days on the cell phone.
Let's meet again you say
when you have a free moment.

And then you find them in the air,
ghosts replaying their heartbreaks,
particles of dust breaking down
in the red rays of light shooting
through the window.
Old friends call you with new problems
that are really old problems,
chronicling their family histories
and diseases, pinning down
each significant moment for posterity.

How long can you listen?
How long can they talk?

Old friends remember
what you would like to forget.
They hug you
as though each hug will be the last.
Old friends knock on wood,
keep their fingers crossed,
toss a little salt to the wind,
We wish you the best of luck, they say.
You'll need it.

Pretenders

She pretended to be Cinderella, dressed in rags, sweeping the ashes from the hearth. I lay down at her feet as she tickled my nose with her feather duster, and then swept it over my body. "Not clean enough," I said and tore off her rags. Her breasts sponged my face and chest and then she finished me off, clean as a whistle.

I pretended to be a wild boar in lordosis, my rump lifted high in the air, digging up white truffles. She smelled the musk, brushed off the truffles and ate them. Then she couldn't resist my advances, her body ovulating.

She pretended to be an orchid with purple blossoms, breathing in the humid air. Her perfume lingered, but I didn't dare touch her because her branch was frail and her blossoms would fall.

I pretended to be a lion, prowling the savannah. She hid in the grass, but I smelled her fear and drove her into the open, where she ran from me. When I caught her, I forced her to the ground, lording over her, tearing her clothes, causing the blood to flow. "Not so rough," she snapped.

"But I'm a lion," I answered, "and you're my prey." Then she lay still in the weeds as though already dead, which meant that I could do what I wanted with her and did, though she wouldn't look at me or even pretend to feel anything.

She pretended to be a vampire bat and gripped the lintel, hanging in the doorframe. "Bats hang upside down," I said.

"Not this bat," she replied. Her long tongue flicked out, catching a fly. She swallowed it whole and then did it again. I watched her from across the room, but didn't come any closer because I feared her razor sharp teeth and long wings, though her body was silky.

I pretended to be a window, causing her to skitter around the room to avoid burning up in my light. She found a shadow in the corner and clung to it until dusk. Then she pretended to be a large jagged rock and let out a big shout, but before she could hurl herself into me, I changed again, wrapping her up, clinging to her rough edges while she rolled me over and over.

Not Babs

When I woke up after my nap, Babs was not Babs, my girl
of the cherry lip balm, icing her lips every ten minutes and
then puckering, my girl clicking her long purple nails on the
counters, my girl of the burning tips and the glossy eyes,
fan of Katy Perry, jumping up and down like a California
Gurl whenever the MTV video comes on, Babs of the
white flowers and black hair, my Babs, my broad-faced
babe singing the sparrows into flight with her hoarse voice,
my Babs spreading her joy to the crows lined up like kids
waiting for a free scoop of Ben & Jerry's. But if Babs was not
Babs, she was not Ginger either, her best friend querulous
as a gaggle of geese. She was not Hester, her fat cousin
sour and dour, like a tongue coated with the residue from
too many Starbursts. Babs was not her friend Nico, not
mysterious and savory, imprinting her scent in the mind of
every man she sleeps with.

When I woke up after my nap, Babs was Barbara, slender
and taller looking, large brown eyes, the clock ticking
behind her face, Barbara of the creamy blouses and
vanilla walls, Barbara of the good China and the Sterling
Silver, Barbara of the wavy red layers, ready to get down
to business, lighting up the quiz rooms with her chatter,
chatting up the bosses, scrolling down the aisles, zeroing
in on the bright billboards, loading apps like bullets,
Barbara digging up rocks and earth, ripping weeds and
honeysuckles out of the soil, calling for backup like a movie
cop who's tracked down the kingpin of a drug-dealing
operation, Barbara glorying in the glaze of peonies and
lilies, but also Barbara of the "Let's make it snappy," snappy

the kitchen clean up, snappy scrubbing the dried pee off the toilet, windexing the mirrors clean of the white splotches flicked off the electric toothbrush, Barbara surfing the flat screen channels relentlessly, snappy calling it a day and a night, whistling the wizard out of the tree, braising the brazen rooster, no more basking in the honey field, no more sliding down the sheets, no more happy carnage—snappy, snappy, snappy . . .

Flurry

My lover and I disagreed about where to keep the baby. She
flew into a flurry of snow. "Enough already," I said. In the
other room, the baby cried. The snow melted in my hair and
on my forehead, drops running down my face. The snow
was sticking to the floor. "I want the baby *where* and *when*
I want the baby," she said. "But the baby is ours," I said and
stood my ground over by the coffee table. "Only in name," she
answered, her flurries waning. "I'm the mommy." The baby
cried louder. I closed the window. "You're a flurry of snow," I
said, "no two ways about it." She rose into a bright whiteness.
"My baby is a bundle of snow," she said, rocking him back
and forth. Now I began to shiver. When I turned the heat
up, gusts of snow blew against my face and body, blinding
me until I pulled out my snow goggles. The room went dark
for a second. That's when the crying stopped.

About the Ears

In the mirror my ears stick out
as though trying to communicate
with the tip of my nose.
Blond tendrils sprout
along the edges, sometimes
buried by the hair sticking out
over my ears, sometimes
wiring out on their own
to catch a kiss tingling the air
or the song playing on a noisy cell phone.
Should I cut them off at the root
and risk them coming back, darker,
stronger like an army out for revenge
or should I let them grow out
until they wag like divining rods?
The hair on my Uncle Jack's ears
stuck up like the teeth of a comb
and spiders curled on the rim
of Miss Ledbetter's lobes,
the fourth grade teacher who sentenced
me to a month in the janitor's closet.
As always, my ears won't put up
with too much history or reflection.
Hungry for gossip, they order me
out of the bathroom, impatient
to get on the phone. When Brenda
unloads her packet of secrets,
"Can I be frank?" whispering
like thighs brushing cloth,
my ears flush with warmth

pleased that my predictions
have all come true. They perk up
when voices come up the road
or when the dog leaps off the couch,
barking and circling under the window.
But now they are a little irritable
because the mice scratch messages
betraying their household
and the mound of dirt reappears
where the chipmunk is digging his cave
and the pink orchids carry on
their affair as if no one is listening.

Good Sense

"Daven" comes from "divine,
and what's more divine
than a lovely divan on rollers,

a real holy roller.
If you get on the backside
of a donkey, you'll learn to bray.

Never paddle in a puddle
or peddle your paddle in a river
or split hairs over a fallen petal.

Let the seeds fly
into the bad man's eyes.
Let flax or flux drift

down over the black tuxes.
Weed out the liars at the wedding
and don't marry anyone with bad dishes.

Breaking the Fast

Now that my blessings rot,
now that I get down on my knees
to feed the garden to the worms
my soles yearn for warm water,
a basin. My arches rise
toward the new kingdom,
the camel's striped neck,
the fat man squeezed into the eye
of the needle. The congregation
of crows sings, "I told you so"
and clouds rain burgundy
on lapidary cruisers boating
through damp leaves.
Now that I'm a nation of stinks,
a wilderness of fetid flowers,
the fete goes full tilt
after midnight. The Vet
sings soprano at the piano,
melting the hearts of his horses.
Lacy black panties drop
like dollar bills, and firm brown
bottoms lift the horizon,
a mountain of moons, giving
new meaning to the old saw,
"20-20 hindsight." Now that
I've grown two heads,
it's easy to spot duplicity,
hustling around the corner,
and crossing the street is a breeze.
I lick the pearly bud and cry out

for more. The fish listen
swimming in gold vats.
The flowers wink at glowering
rabbis, glistening like wet
vases. I hear orgasms
coming into their own, singing
like children in angry choirs,
The fast is over.

Philanthropist

Give something back,
some rakes and shovels
for the decimated villages, a few
tents, packs of matches,
some coupons for the grocery
blown away years ago,
cases of bottled water,
basketball jerseys, old shoes,
some broken computers.
Give back a few free tickets
to a concert, a night out on the town
for a lucky couple. Call in a few favors.
Get the power turned back on
for one day. Get the celebration going,
the carousels circling the cities
of tents, the homeless dancing
in open sewers. Call your
dwarf planets. Get them to
airlift boxes of dust.
Give something back
from your castle overlooking the ocean,
from your loft over the fancy boulevard,
from your personal jet, carrying
a cargo of clouds. Give something
back from the center of your sun,
from your many channels and satellites,
from your glorious galaxy on the Web.
Create new foundations
and charities. Cut the ribbon
to begin another building project.

Get down on your knees
and plant the seeds that'll
destroy all other seeds.

First Snow

The first snow falls, perfect
white flakes. The dogs
sniff it, bury their noses,
kick it up. Kids cheer,
open their mouths to the sky
to taste it. Red balloons
float toward clouds. The snow
comes down in threads, filaments,
short, clear sentences.
Windows shine. Siding glitters.
Crows on birch branches
shake it from their wings.
Turkeys waddle through it, bumping
rear ends. The snow smoothes
the wrinkles from our faces,
makes us laugh, our cheeks
red. The snow falls,
and some pretend to ski
across a white plain
and some imagine sledding
down long white hills
and some tumble in it
and some lie down in it.
Later the snow'll mound
against windows, pile against
glass storm doors,
hump into jagged hills.
Later it'll snap branches, fell
trees. Later it'll turn mean,
pitted by rocks, sand, salt,

blinding the eyes of drivers
and tipping over cars.
Then, it'll grow heavy with slush
and mud. But for now,
the first snow falls
and everyone is happy.

Crow

The crow came to our door, wings covered in mud. We took him in, cleaned him off, fed him a good dinner. "Crows can predict the future," Anna claimed. "Let's ask him to tell us what he knows." Not now—he's in shock. The crow propped himself on the arm of the couch. "He seems fine to me," Anna replied. He preened his feathers until they were black and shiny. "If a crow stays in your house, you'll find a fortune where you least expect it," he said. "Sounds good to me," I responded, but Anna had doubts. "Crows are harbingers of death," she said. The crow scoffed at her. "Both of you will live long lives," he said. "It's in the genes." But the crow had a dark look in his eyes that belied his prophecy. "Tell us the truth," Anna insisted. She walked to the door and opened it. "Or leave." After the crow flew out, we gathered a bundle of his feathers and kept them in a glass jar. "A crow's feathers can protect us against bad luck," she said as if wishing it were true. "Never trust a crow," I said, but soon we parted, fearing the worst.

Give It Up

Give up the dragons tattooed on your arms
in blue and red, your proud captions
in green, "Fight for yourself. . . . Make it
Right. . . . Stand for something or nothing."
Give up waiting your turn, because no one
gets a turn unless he takes it. Give up
the constellations, which are always
here and always missing, the stars
televising their own deaths, the saturnine
stages, the coy curtains falling
on stubbled stems, desolate decapitations,
while sylvan stogies smoke into eternity.
Give up Cassiopeia and the seven sisters,
your bouts with the moon, the wrestling matches
in the dust. Give up the dust for more dust,
the salt for whatever you've lost,
what you've already lost for what you're going to lose.
Give up the hawk that roosts in the mirror,
the bobcat pouncing on its prey, the angels
nodding on their stalks, the blue space
between what you see and what you don't.
Give up regret and your desire to do good,
because desire is nothing but absence—
oil spews from pipes in the ocean,
cash burns up pockets and countries.
Give up the fierce flies, the fey
spirit at the bottom of your glass. Give up
the old man rattling off his heroic deeds,
railing about deceit and vanity, he is deceit
and vanity. Give up salt, the herb garden,